Literature written for young adults...

by young adults.

Allow yourself to be surprised.

My Own Words

Young Writers Chapbook Series

Jamal Clay

VERBALEYZE
Press

Atlanta

Cover artwork © 2013 by Susan Arauz Barnes
Editing by Derek Koehl and Tavares Stephens
ISBN: 978-0-9856451-7-5

VerbalEyze Press books are available at special discounts for bulk purchases in the United States by corporations, institutions and other organizations.

For information, address VerbalEyze Press, 1376 Fairbanks Street SW, Atlanta, Georgia 30310.

VerbalEyze does not participate, endorse, or have any authority or responsibility concerning private correspondence between our authors and the public. All mail addressed to authors are forwarded, but the publisher cannot, unless specifically instructed by the author, give out an address or phone number.

VerbalEyze Press
A division of VerbalEyze, Inc.
www.verbaleyze.org

Mom, Kamyra, Auntie, Grandma,
I want to thank you.
I would have no reason to write
if not for your influence and encouragement.
So thank you.

– Jamal

Table of Contents

My Own Words

Foreword

Many a black and white speckled notebook has been privy to the growing pains of young artists. They sketch, narrate, poet and rhyme to make sense of the world and orient themselves to the gravitational pull of coming of age. But their musings beg for answers and an empathetic head nod, so YaHeard? Poetics was born.

Whether speaking heartache at the mic, spitting social commentary over tracks or texting observations into the ether, the power and influence of word is undeniable and YaHeard? Poets study the craft, explore their creative process and learn how to promote their artistic endeavors through collaborations with organizations like VerbalEyze, a beacon for young artists.

YaHeard? was founded by Educator-Artists to support the creative stirrings of tweens and teens and the publication of this chapbook honors and encourages the work of a young artists whose passion and talent confirms them as part of a new generation of prolific writers, artists and musicians. Their musings have escaped from first notebooks and into your hands. Answer if you dare; head nod if you must ---this young scribe dares to explore the power of voice.

Ya Heard?

Susan Arauz Barnes
Co-founder, YaHeard? Poetics

Editors' Note

The Young Writers Chapbook Series is an expression of the mission and vision that is core to what we do at VerbalEyze. Through this series, we are able to provide talented, emerging young authors their debut introduction to the reading public. We are grateful that you also share an enthusiasm for young authors and the vibrant and energized perspectives they bring to our shared understanding of the human experience and what it means to live, love, long, lose and wonder as we travel together through this world.

We are pleased to bring to you an exceptional young writer, Jamal Clay, with this edition of the Young Writers Chapbook. We trust that you will be as engaged and challenged by her words as we have been. Jamal is part of an exceptional group of young writers, YaHeard? Poetics. He and his fellow writers are an never-ending encouragement and inspiration to us.

Read, enjoy and, as always, *allow yourself to be surprised.*

Derek Koehl
Tavares Stephens

I Can Do Anything

I can write a rap

I can make a beat

There's nothing stopping these feet

From traveling the world

With no map

All I do is write raps

I don't copy

I paste

With my own words

I make

The spectacular

From what I face

That's why I'm winning

This race

Follow Me

Follow the light

You see that's right

I don't want no pain

I don't want to fight

You go to school

And use the dictionary

I'm an artist

I use Pictionary

While I'm here

I make my mark

You think it's easy

A walk in the park

But you don't understand

The trouble I go through

To make a start

Let's rewind and bring it back

It's hard work now that's a fact

New skills

New game

Nothing separates artists

The poor; the fame

Both have the same dream

Give sweat, tears and blood

The thing that separates them

Is none of the above

Jamal Clay

Future

False information

Got new keys

And a brand new station

Got my college degree

My mom and my dad

So proud of me

I'm going to adulthood

New car, new job, new life

Doing so well

Can't mock the beat

You can try to catch me

But I'm on my longest streak

Now I'm on the beach

I walk along the shore

Feel sand on my feet

Never been to a beach before

Now dreaming of the highest mountain

And the mountain's peak

But right now I'm here

And I've got the right

To live without fear

Sometimes I'm in headlights

A boy like a deer

Believe me when I tell you

That that's a true fatality

Time to stop dreaming

And switch back

To reality

Jamal Clay

Discipline

Discipline

Dedication

Determination

I'm making

My own path with my own expectations

But people start to lose their head

Look ahead

And copy someone else instead

I made my own path

So I'ma go ahead

And walk on it instead

I'm going to my future

As a song writer

And a producer

They say I'm crazy

But they're the ones acting clueless

Get a brain and use it

Or you'll be left behind

If you want to catch up, bro

You've got to use your mind

Ice Cream

Ice cream

Ice cream

Cherry on top

We got the new boyz here

And the old ones down the block

Old boyz got the afro and the box cut

And the old boyz

Told the new boyz

Said you better

Keep your mouth shut

The new ones

Got offended

Started joking

But they meant it

The old boyz started recognizing

All the things they invented

From the slang

To the silver chain

To the rigidity chain

The old boyz walked away

New boyz made their fame

'Til the old boyz came back
Dressed in skinny jeans

My Generation

I've got the feeling

Of desperation

Not used to being here

Sitting and waiting

That's what's wrong with my generation

Doing late homework

Procrastinating

We are independent

We do it our selves

We care about food

But not about health

We say we can't wait for our first car

Bills are brought up

There's one big silence

Come with me

And we'll decide

If we face the world

Or stand beside it

Want a challenge

It's just been provided

Bully

It's no use
They've got their hand
Over your mouth
Shutting you up
Your real friends
Can't hear you
They only see you
Betrayal
Betrayal
A clique
Likes to tease the individuals
It's in their body language
You were once invisible
Don't act like you don't know
What I'm talking bout
Fooled by the fake friends
Who you're hanging out with
You want to scream and shout
But it's no use
They've got their hand
Over your mouth

Shutting you up

Your real friends

Can't hear you

They only see you

Traitor

Traitor

Jamal Clay

Problems

Let's talk about you and mom

And sis

Let's talk about this

It's not about me

I'm here to talk about you

Not to thank you

I'm here to tell you

What I think is true

Look in my eyes

Tell me why

You think I forgive

When you don't provide

You said you'd take a break

From my kind

I think seven years

Has been enough time

I don't want no sorry

Don't apologize

Just fix your mistakes

Make a promise to God

Text me on a BlackBerry

If that's too scary

Call me up

Excuses

Excuses

Yo, papa

Deuces

But you come back

Making a promise

Seven years ago

Man you should've

Been honest

Turned your back

And never turned around

Don't come running toward

This family

You've given up your crown

Shake It Off

I get up and shake it off

Make and shape my future

With or without help

I'll make it

No tutors

Whatever goods I find at the top

I'll use to help others

The only person

Around to teach me that

Was my mother

She cooks she cleans

I'm sure she's fed up

With excuses

Is he really messed up in the brain?

Or are his marriage ideals useless

The Past

I can worry about the past

And just let it take over me

Or face it

And tell myself

That's just history

I'm the man of the house now

My dad didn't stay

Went off with this other lady

With child support he couldn't pay

There's always an excuse

To why he didn't show up today

He's not going to come at all

Either this or that way

Only a dummy would do one thing wrong

And try it the same way again

Jamal Tywon Clay is a twelve year old who wants to be a producer, writer, and rapper. Jamal started writing when he was nine years old. He was inspired by rapper, producer and entrepreneur, Jay-Z. Whenever his song was on the radio, his mom would pause it and explain the lyrics. This inspired Jamal to get his own message out. Jamal writes song and rap lyrics and he is inspired by uplifting songs like, "Too Late to Apologize" by One Republic and "On Top of the World" by Imagine Dragons.

Jamal feels most creative when he hears a song that makes him want to dance and smile. It makes him want to start writing *immediately*!

He attends the Ron Clark Academy in East Point, GA. He lives in Atlanta, Georgia and attends the Ron Clark Academy in East Point, Georgia. Jamal has a loving mother and sister and appreciates the stories of truth that his family has passed down to him.

Photo credit: J. Amezqua

VERBALEYZE
Press

Empowering young writers to say, "I am my scholarship!"

Open call for submissions to the
Young Writers Anthology!

See your work in print!

Become a published writer!

**Earn royalites that can help
you pay for college!s**

VerbalEyze Press is accepting submissions from young adult writers, ages 13 to 22, in any of the following genres:

- poetry
- short story
- songwriting
- playwriting
- graphic novel
- creative non-fiction

For submission details, visit
www.verbaleyze.org

VerbalEyze serves to foster, promote and support the development and professional growth of emerging young writers.

VERBALEYZE
Writers Cooperative

VerbalEyze is a nonprofit organization whose mission is to foster, promote and support the development and professional growth of emerging young writers.

The *Young Writers Anthology* is published as a service of VerbalEyze in furtherance of its goal to provide young writers with access to publishing opportunities that they otherwise would not have.

Fifty percent of the proceeds received from the sale of the *Young Writers Anthology* are paid to the authors in the form of scholarships to help them advance in their post-secondary education.

For more information about VerbalEyze and how you can become involved in its work with young writers, visit www.verbaleyze.org.

www.ingramcontent.com/pod-product-compliance
Lightning Source LLC
Chambersburg PA
CBHW032103040426
42449CB00007B/1171